OTHERNESS

To Ron:
Thank you
for your
support!

M. Ayodele Heath

OTHERNESS

Poems by M. Ayodele Heath

Cover Art: "Drained" from "Ode to Hands" series by Lisa Chalian-Rock
Brick Road logo by Dwight New

Library of Congress Control Number: 2010942351
ISBN-13: 978-0-9841005-4-5
ISBN-10: 0-9841005-4-7

Published by Brick Road Poetry Press
P. O. Box 751
Columbus, GA 31902-0751
www.brickroadpoetrypress.com

Acknowledgements

Earlier versions of these poems have appeared in the following journals and anthologies:

Callaloo: "Day Negative 7"

Chattahoochee Review: "Conjuring the Whole Note," "On a Fieldtrip to the Botanical Gardens, Kenya Gets a Lesson (Not in the Lesson Plan)"

Crab Orchard Review: "The Dreamlife of Dr. Bledsoe's Inner Pickaninny"

diode: "Dusk of the Afrikaner," "A Brief History of Okra (Master's Take)"

Dorothy Sargent Rosenberg Annual Poetry Prize 2009: "South Africa: 25 Exposures"

Eclectic Literary Forum: "On Closing Woodruff Park, Atlanta (for renovations for the 1996 Summer Olympics)"

InMotion Magazine: "A Sharecropper's Pantoum"

International Gallerie (India): "Unmanifesto (Notes on Post-postcolonialism, a 3rd Draft in CP Time)"

Java Monkey Speaks Anthology, Volume II (Poetry Atlanta Press, 2005): "On a Fieldtrip to the Jim Crow Museum, Kenya Learns (the Meaning of No)"

Mississippi Review: "A Sharecropper's Pantoum"

My South: A People, a Place, a World All Its Own, ed. Robert St. John and Bryan Curtis (Rutledge Hill Press, 2005): "Home"

Mythium: "Once, During an Eclipse, I Happened to Look into the Sun," "The Veil," "Lovesong at the End of the World," "An Everyday God"

New Millennium Writings: "Eye of the Beholder"

The New York Quarterly: "Metachromasis," "The Token's Final Word (on Being Asked to Provide the Black Perspective in Class)"

Open City: "Uncle Charlie Comes to da Family Reunion"

RHINO: "The Stuttering House Negro Diviner Speaks: Byrd Plantation, 1863"

storySouth: "The Tragic Mulatto, or One Drop Rule Hits the Silver Screen"

***

Special thanks to the Caversham Centre for Writers & Artists in Balgowan, Kwazulu Natal, South Africa & the Fulton County Arts Council for the residency, enabling the creation of "South Africa: 25 Exposures" and "Dusk of the Afrikaner."

CONTENTS

I.

II.

III.

But I see what it is, you are not from these parts, you don't know what our twilights can do. Shall I tell you?

—Pozzo, from Samuel Beckett's *Waiting for Godot*

I.

Etymology of Ain't

Ain't
used to be *an't*
which comes from
am not as in   *I ain't you*
but also *is not* as in   *He ain't me*
& also *have not* as in   *I ain't been*
                                                        and don't wanna be

Ain't is a state of that which is not
Ain't is a state in the American South
Ain't country, *ain't* hip-hop
Ain't nappy, *ain't* cornrows, *ain't* dreadlocks
Ain't ignores dress codes   no shoes, no socks
Ain't wears no drawers   don't own any

Ain't ain't never apologized for being
Ain't never been apologetic
Some say ain't no future in *ain't*
& *ain't* ain't what it used to be
but where *ain't* is, *is* ain't
Ain't *ain't* metaphysical?

Is you *is* or is you *ain't?* I ain't no haint

Ain't never been three-fifths of nothing

Ain't trying to be no more than I am

I is whole

Before I was born I was all

They placed *ain't*'s tombstone between *'tis* and *'twas*

But *ain't* stands defiantly as *don't* and *won't*

Tar & feather me burn me down

I ain't supposed to be here

But I is

Conjuring the Whole Note

White folks hear the blues come out, but they don't know how it got there.

—Ma Rainey, blues singer

Fingers in piano prayer—long & black, wisps
of dusk, curled at the tips. Be:

Legs of the mosquito, walking silently
(as Jesus) on the starless green water

of the bayou, atop some thing so dark
he dare not disturb it. Tentatively. G...

to A... to B^{b}... Drowned in gin, Papa
Knuckles rides a rickety piano riff down

a back-alley bar off Beale Street, where we burn—
brown, holy, charred. We: Bones

in the bayou, stirring clouds   of mosquitoes
with an open promise of our flesh, by light

of a blazing cross—Godless robes, white
masks. Baptized in the Blues of a man who outlasts

all of this, blue even tinting his

smile. *A Mississippi-cain't-hold-a-whole-Nile*

of blues. Too blue to shoo the mosquito

on his brow: Now draining his

blood. Now draining his very

life

The Dreamlife of Dr. Bledsoe's Inner Pickaninny

Bledsoe, you're a shameless chitterling eater! Ha! And not only do you eat them, you sneak and eat them in private *when you think you're not being observed! ...I accuse you of indulging in a filthy habit, Bledsoe! Lug them out so we can see! I accuse you before the eyes of the world!*

—Invisible Man, from Ralph Ellison's *Invisible Man*

Though he long ago resumed consuming pork,

to this day he still will not eat fried chicken

in front of white folk (Octoroons,

or even Negroes he needs

to impress). Pondering entrées

at a recent business lunch, craving the crunchy,

peppered crust, his glands moisten

at the mere thought.

But he fears

the Black skillet's neon grease will wildly distort

the innate thickness of his lips. That sucking a drum-

stick dry will expose the enormous

ivory bone stuck through his nose, warping

his face, weighing him down in an apelike walk

till his meticulous pin-striped life unravels

like an unruly raffia skirt.

Thus, when dessert time comes, he avoids sweet
potato confections, pecan confrontations, and other
denigrating delectables at all costs. Instead,
his controlled fork picks (like a good little
boy) through cool fruit salad. Devouring apples,
cherries, pears and grapes, he leaves a clean White
plate—curiously bare but for
watermelon parts.

Asked why he will not eat them, his reply:
Where would I hide
the seeds?

A Brief History of Okra (Master's Take)

Discovered in her wild state
on the flood-plain of the Nile,
Okra arrived at Port of New Orleans
circa 1700:
Germs stored in a drum.

*

Start Okra from seed. She does not transplant
well. She's best planted
in Southern soil, after all danger
of frost has passed.

*

RULE OF THUMB: Keep them
separated. Okra seeds are large, easy
to handle, but they need
warm weather to grow well.

In Northern climes, you won't have
much of a crop.

*

Picking pods while wet
may darken their skin which
might make them seem bitter
at first. But really, their taste
is unaffected.

*

Unlike her fairer cousin, Cotton,
Okra's showy yellow flower
blooms just one day a year:

Just make sure that day
don't last
too long.

The Tragic Mulatto, or One-Drop Rule Hits the Silver Screen (ca. 1930)

Our brave White hero,

upon unveiling his mulatto

mistress's villainous dark secret,

slices her shadowy wrist,

then,   in the ultimate sacrifice,

pulls it to his quivering mouth

& sucks

        a single drop

of her Negro blood—enough to become

*

a Negro himself! The frenetic *Whites*

Only cinema—half in awe, half in disgust—half

applauds our newly-mulattoed hero & his lover's

fateful walk, hand-in-hand into the darkening

    sunset.

If I could, the green-eyed projectionist thinks,

I would have them

burn

Eye of the Beholder

—after seeing the *Without Sanctuary*† exhibit
Beauty in things exists in the mind which contemplates them.

—David Hume, from *Essays*, "Of Tragedy"

a wave of ten

thousand foaming white

men stormed

a georgia

jail & lynched

a colored boy

in june rain

for a smile (which

he did commit) as he

                    hung

from a yellow traffic

light—noose

bearing all

their weight—not one

said *Stop*, but

        one

took

a picture

†*Without Sanctuary*: James Allen's traveling exhibition of photographs and postcards of lynchings in America.

Metachromasis

With consonants sharp as fangs & clean
as bone, my skin whitens as the hairs

in a leper's sore.   *Behold,* the Good Book says,
he cometh with clouds...   & Presto! Covered

in fluttering doves, I become a sculpture
of birdshit.   My key is C-major as I whistle

inside a picket fence. Backstroking
through a creek of clam chowder, life

is a bowl of shredded coconut. Look, now
I am yodeling while milking a cow!

Bland as rice cake, *yawn* I am boring
even myself. Write me across your blackboard

as Truth: I civilize with my savagery.
I am a foam

which knows no foreign shore.

Dusk of the Afrikaner

Akulanga lashona lingendaba.

—Zulu proverb

I.

1 ONCE UPON A TIME, WHEN TIME was measured in the length of shadows, I met a woman–on a dirt road much like this one—who did not know the smell of rain.

2 *How sad*, she said to no one. *I want to know it.*

3 Her long Zulu eyes were not nearly as long as her gaze, on this day, impossibly February: heat billowing in waves; the once-White sun finally lowering among the aloes, by great pallbearers of Light, into the ground.

4 On the day I met this *umfazi*, I stumbled over her shadow & felt a sudden chill. Sure & black as thunderclouds.

5 Far beyond the townships, beyond rivers of dust with no memory of the sea, her gathering shadow was easily the longest I'd ever seen. It must have been the longest in the world.

6 *As a desert without clouds*, she said. *As a sleep without dreams.*

7 Such a shadow must have meant she was very old. Perhaps, the oldest woman in the world.

8 *But I am not*, she said, as if burning the pages in my eyes.

II.

1 THEN, LIKE A MIGHTY black river of Night, the *umfazi's* shadow fell across the Earth, crushing the aloes & the hills & the trees. & all throughout Zululand, the blackest nightmare of one became the other's dream.

2 & the sky wept.

3 *Like one who has not wept for centuries might weep,* she said. *With the kind of weeping which feels like thunder, which makes the earth shudder, which portends the end of days.*

4 & some ran for shelter. & some ran for the sea. But millions more had waited lifetimes for this storm. Through moon, through sun, they clutched the aching earth.

5 *Till rain & mud,* she said, *became tears & blood.*

6 & there they stood. As ones who have not stood for centuries might stand. *As if standing for something,* she said. As if suddenly aware of the straightness of their own posture.

7 Then they raised their faces like black moonflowers till the whole of Zululand was ablaze with Midnight

8 & stars rained from her tongue—this witness, this poet—so moved she was by their forgotten beauty.

South Africa: 25 Exposures

i.

Arrival in Johannesburg airport:
So many White faces,
I must be in the wrong country.

That is, till I see
the baggage handlers, who all look
just like me.

ii.

STANDARD TIP IS 5 RAND!
the airport sign says, ONLY TIP THOSE
WEARING ORANGE VESTS!

iii.

Ahhh, Zulu is a sound
for sore ears: Soft. Percussive.
Music. *Click-Click!*

when spoken. For example
ngqongqoza, has two
clicks & means

to knock. *Ngqongqosha* has two
too & means to carry a child
on one's shoulders.

iv.

To stand so tall,
yet balance so much:
a woman's work.

v.

Such bright scarves sing
as they are beaten
against the rocks.

vi.

Yebo, Mr. Cow,
Are you coming or going
down this dirt road?

vii.

End of the day,
25 kilometres home: Left.
Right. Left. Right. Left.

viii.

Night here is so dark
I can't even see
my own skin.

ix.

The skyline's teeth
will swallow your eyes!
the sangoma sez.

x.

<IMAGE DESTROYED>

xi.

As he flaps among the clouds,
the shrike's magical tail
kisses the acacia trees.

xii.

There goes
another lion:
Yawning.

xiii.

This Xhosa girl is taught
not to look
me in the eye,

Oh, but when she sings
I feel the floor
rise.

xiv.

Where have all the diamonds
gone? Certainly not
on her black hands.

xv.

When he leaves for the mines,
the moon is full. It will fill again
before he returns.

xvi.

BIGGER! STRONGER! LONGER!
the witchdoctor's promise—
even here.

xvii.

This woman with bare breasts
looks like she has
something to say:

Amandla, or
I will not die
of AIDS.

xviii.

Zululand
is greener than
even Ireland:

No wonder
they came
& would not leave.

xix.

Tea time for one
means work time
for the other.

xx.

Another expired goldmine,
another horizon of ghetto:
WELCOME TO SOWETO

xxi.

Radio deejays transmit
in eleven different languages:
What a wild dial!

*

With my two left feet,
can you teach me
the latest township dance?

xxii.

Chakalaka tastes
just like it sounds:
Boommmmmmmmmm

xxiii.

EUROP ANS ONLY
The letters on this bench
have faded from use.

xxiv.

Zulu lightning show:
How does the sky rumble so
& not fall apart?

xxv.

Named for apartheid's architect,
Verwoerd Ave. still runs
through the heart

of Johannesburg.

Some Other Place, or Masks

[T]his thing that is the heaviest thing of all my years, is the heaviest thing of all your years also.

—Alan Paton, *Cry, the Beloved Country*

African/American

in Pietermaritzburg,

toy-drummed & faux-speared,

I hunted for a souvenir

to bring to you

from Mother,

a half-world away

*

Stalking the aisles

in canvas shorts

& cotton shirt

a full month in,

I held the tongue

which betrayed me before

secretly hoping

my skin

would be enough

camouflage

*

So when
an elder, posing
as cashier—
not in Zulu, but
in English—asked
Where are you from?
my heart   dropped
like the KwaNogqaza
Falls.

*

My clothes? My neck? My nose? My ears?
What was it? I wondered aloud

What mark, this time   had
in fact, betrayed me?

*

Your walk   He said
You walk upright.
South African men
don't walk so straight.

You walk proud,

so I knew   you

were from some other place

like Nigeria

Neckrollology

The most venomous snake

in all of Africa is not the black mamba,

though it does come from

the depths of the Congo, pulled deep

from the arch in her back, deep from hand

on hip, winding & winding, wound

up, whip-

lash—reptilian

stance of one about to

strike something. Make space: This

is a cosmic conjure of ancient name like

Zanzibar, Zambia, or Mozambique, which left the Greeks

baffled by its geometry. Its improvised axis

is jazz, falls between

3rd & 4th dimensions. Angular rotation: 720

degrees. Rotational speed: 45 revolutions

per minute. She spun it & spun it

out

of control, a neckroll:

If I had wanted a double

cheeseburger, I would have ordered a double

cheeseburger. How the hell did you get
double cheeseburger
from two-piece snack?

The Token's Final Word (on Being Asked to Provide the Black Perspective in Class)

I speak for all Black people
when I say this:

I do not speak
for all

Black people.

II.

On a Fieldtrip to the Botanical Gardens, Kenya Gets a Lesson (Not in the Lesson Plan)

If she could, she would choose

to be the color of Yellow cosmos, French lavender,

Texas paintbrush (or a Shasta daisy at the very

least): *Anything but the color of pots*

& kettles! Which she is. Which is when

a chaperone, who also happens

to be her Mother, rebuts: But Kenya,

you are also the color of Night,

whose beauty cannot even be contained

by Earth, nor expanding galaxies, wandering

exquisitely as the thoughts of God. The color

of Infinity, if it had one; of Eternity,

if it ever paused to be measured. My daughter,

you are the dream where God made Earth's first

black volcanic beaches, whose undulating soot

would birth cosmos and lavender and paintbrush,

but whose first bloom was you: a hue

so divine and heavy, no lesser flower
could bear it.

On a Fieldtrip to the Jim Crow Museum, Kenya Learns (the Meaning of No)

Here is a gavel no Negro ever struck.

Over here, a first-base no Negro ever reached.

Here is a bus seat no Negro ever took

And here, a pulpit where no Negro ever preached.

Here is a ballot no Negro ever cast.

Over here, a lunch counter where no Negro was ever fed.

Here, a threshold no Negro has ever crossed.

And here, burial soil that never touched no Negro dead.

Here is a diving board no Darkie ever used.

Over here, a payphone no Pickaninny ever used.

Here, a Coca Cola machine no Coon ever used.

And here, the swearing Bible:

No Negro. Will Never. Use.

Here is a water fountain to never wet no Negro lips.

Now here, a toilet where no Negro ever sit.

Here, a textbook no Negro has ever read,

Filled with a knowledge

no Nigger will ever get.

Genealogy of the Byrd Family

My Mama maiden name is Byrd. Word is

da name came from my

Great-

     Great-

          Great-

Granddaddy Junie,

who useta catch da Holy Ghost

     in da cottonfields

spinnin round & spreadin

his

     long

          black

               arms,

wide like wings against da sky—

Dey say like dat eagle

who teach the angels how to fly

                       Hallelujah!

*

But Big Mama Sadie say, *Unh, unh,*

Dat name come from

Great-

    Great-

        Great-

            Great Auntie Boo, *who*
useta lead da worksongs in da cane *fields*
with a soprano so high&sweet
she made da bluest hummingbirds dance
& da greenest cane lean down & weep
rivers of brown sugar

                      Sweet Jesus!

*

But Big Uncle Toonkie say, *Naw, naw, naw*
Dat name come from
Great-

    Great-

        Great-

            Great-Grandpapa Adika
who on da ninety-ninth lash in da ricefield
finally fell to his knees before da overseer
turned east toward Africa

                Glory
sprouted wings like a sankofa[†]

                Oh glory!

42

rose toward Freedom

&jus flew away!

Good God Almighty!

*

Dat's what dey say.

But da truth of da matter

is dat Byrd come to us

from a Carolina slavemasta

who folk in England ran dis ol' country inn

dat for generations came to be known

da whole kingdomwide

for dey collection of exotic African birds

which *never* flew,

but which dey kept

caged-up inside

[†]*sankofa*: a bird of Ghanian mythology whose head faces the opposite direction of its body so that, even as it advances, its eye is constantly on its past. From Akan, translated literally: *One must return to the past to move forward.*

The Stuttering House Negro Diviner Speaks:
Byrd Plantation, 1863

A ch-ch-ch-charge

A ch-ch-ch-charge

A ch-ch-ch-charge to keep I have

A charge   I have to keep

and f-f-f-fit it for   the charge shall move in

    us

    us orbit around

    around the around the

    charge   becomes

    b-b-b-becomes greater

    b-b-b-becomes greater:

Still   Not

Still   Greater than

    Greater than

    this?

{Cross-

fade}   Nothing is greater than

{Cross-

fade}   It-it-it

don't stop   It-it-it

don't stop   It-it-it

don't stop

da b-b-b-body {*Trans-*

form}   Be-

ware. Beware the power. Be-

ware the power of each

bond: Sh-sh-sh-

shackle

H-h-h-

Handcuff   Sh-sh-sh-

shackle

H-h-h-

Headspin   Sh-sh-sh-

shackle

H-h-h-

Halo   Sh-sh-sh-

Shhhhhhhhhhhh....

                    ***

                              Waters {*Trans-*

form} *erry-erry-erz*

                              Windmill {Trans-

form} Wat- *erry-erry-erz*

Running   *I've known*

R-r-r-running   *Uprock*

Can't keep   running   *My soul*

y-y-yes   *My soul*

R-r-r-running

It do   y-y-yes   *and fit it for the*

sk-sk-sk   I————

***

am mixed

Re-   mixed. Am mixed

Re-   mixed. Am

Re-

erry-re- er-re re-re-re-   Am

erry-re- er-re re-re-re-   Am

erry-re- er-re re-re-re- Re-   leased

leased

leased

leased

*Contains samples from "A Charge to Keep I Have" written by Charles Wesley; "Rappin Blow" written & performed by Kurtis Blow; "The Negro Speaks of Rivers" written by Langston Hughes; "Bridge Over Troubled Waters" written by Paul Simon & performed by Aretha Franklin; "Runnin'" written & performed by The Pharcyde

Things My Father Gave Me (Which I Never Asked For)

—after Jamaica Kincaid's *Girl*

1   Life. A home plate. A backyard with a pitching mound. A split-finger fastball, a slider, a curve. How to break in a glove. When to slide head first. A family name to uphold. Open arms.

2   Time. A Huffy Bike. How to crack pecans. A sandbox. How to piss. How to be a rock. When to till the Earth. How to make a fist. When to fight, when to smile. How to trap a rabbit. How to catch a liar. How to speak when White people are present. (How to talk when White folk ain't.) The difference between a flathead, a Phillips head, and a hard head. A roof over my head. Room to grow.

3   How to shoot a free throw. When to call a foul. How to drive. A high-top fade. How to ask out a lady, how to let her be a woman. How to use a level. How to keep your cool. When to be cool. Cool.

4   A pimpstroll. How to smoke out wasps. Where to get good fish. *Funk & Wagnalls*. When to ask for help, when to give it. How to speak up. A love of brown. Talbotton. How to

mow the lawn, to hammer, to saw. How to change a tire, when to change the oil, how to handle change.

5   How to tie a tie. How to buy a suit. How to earn an honest dollar. How to lead, how to follow. How to read the spread. When to swallow your pride. How to raise a fence. How to use a knife for a pencil sharpener. When to shoot a gun.

6   How to shake a man's hand. How to look him in the eye. A thirst to learn. A book case. Muscadines. Nights to dream. Dreambooks. Reasons to cry. Dark skin. Strong teeth. Full lips. Blood. Two brothers. How to care for elders. How to honor them. How to admit when you're wrong. How to apologize before the funeral. How to love—yes—and how to always come Home.

Home

This is a place where when tomorrow's Easter Sunday &

you ain't got no money, the barber tell ya *Boy, you*

betta get up in this chair & don't even look at you

funny & y'all still listen to the Braves on that same

A.M. radio he heard Hank break Babe record back

in 1974

Where old folks on the front porch with they gold teeth

laughin is like the sweet sweet sound of the gates of

Heaven swingin

& uncles trim they frontyard hedges wavin to every car that

passes by & *Last time I seen you, boy, you was *this* high*

& Grandmas knit rainbows to hang across the sky

A place clownin, Jamesbrownin, *Heyyyyyyyy* into a broom, of

slow-draggin with a mop, Cleopatra Jones in my

arms, or a towel around my head daydreamin I'm a

Supreme

A place of first feels and first kisses and those ol school

whoopins where ya pick your own switches, of

afterschool visits to the Candy Lady— sour apple

Blow Pops & saltwater taffy, Nehi Peach & RC Cola

A place of broken arms & scraped knees & tomboys
climbin crabapple trees, of Stay-Sof-Fro for nappy
heads & the Boogieman hidin beneath the bed, of 4-
Square, hopscotch, red-light-green-light, double-
dutch, and ain't much happenin but that don't stop
the gossips from gatherin for iced tea after church

A place of givin up your seat to the elderly on the bus, of
when a lady's in the room no gentleman would cuss,
of streetlights—not clocks—tellin us when it's dark,
of sittin still when it's thunderin lettin God do His
work

A place passin somebody walkin on the street— whether
you know 'em or not—you know enough to speak,
where your word is your bond and on Sunday shoes
shine like a good family name

A place of no Christmas unless shakin every box under the
tree, of no New Years unless collard greens & black-
eyed peas, of no spring without crowds cheerin the
grand slam & no summer without the Ice Cream
Man

A place of Sunday rides, weekend fish frys, sweet potato
  pies, hoecakes, macaroni & cheese, candied yams
  and fried green tomatoes, mashed potatoes, peach
  cobbler, and sweet hickory ribs so tender they just
  slide off the bone

This is a place
This is a place
This is a place called Home

Afternoon Breezes

—for John Wesley Byrd

Grandfather sits outdoors—
alone—
on his tall, wooden front steps,
which, once upon a time, he built—
in his yellowed, white tee-shirt,
the same he wore yesterday
and the day before that
in the suffocating, south Georgia heat,
Cause it's cooluh out heeyuh
Dan in duh house.

Sweat trickles down
his wrinkled forehead.
Beads trace the bent form
of his back, as he sits—
old, fragile, frail.
Listening to the electric buzz of cicadas,
staring at the maturing sky,
feeling the grass grow yellow
and die.

Five steps up he sits—
so high, he has to climb down.
If he falls, he will die,
but he sits there anyway
for the duration of the dry season,
because it makes him happy
to reminisce about Spring's
vivid pink azalea blooms,
even though they are now shriveled
and dry.

Veins visible, bones contending with skin
at every joint, he hums a hymn he learned
during the Depression.
Aching, arthritic, he climbs down one step
and it creaks
as he wonders when was the last time
he heard Goldie's wind chimes.

The blazing, white sun rides high overhead
as he daydreams of Grandma
and those afternoon breezes,
rolling the frosty glass of lemonade
across his wrinkled forehead
watching the pines sway.

Uncle Charlie Comes to da Family Reunion

Ol' Uncle Charlie shocked everybody
When he showed up to da reunion
With his new wife, Dolly.

Now, it wasn't so much her sunflowery dress,
Nor dat she was tall as a tree.
It was she couldn'ta been no Whiter
If she was first kin to Robert E. Lee!

Goldie stopped midrock in her rockin' chair,
Da chirrun gawked and gaped in surprise,
Pops couldn't even deal da next hand of Tonk,
And all da women kept cuttin dey eyes—

Dat is till dey got a taste o' ol' Dolly
Sweet sweet potato pie!

Mama Mabry Remarks on Brown v. Board of Education 50 Years Later (at Commencement, Booker T. Washington High School, Atlanta)

If this is integration,

then I must be blind

Coz my granddaughter graduatin class

look blacker than mine!

An Everyday God

I.

IT HAS BEEN SAID that God rides
the #98 daily, in a knit pumpkin shawl
when the weather is cool, from Her job at The Beautiful
on Sweet Auburn, where, for the past thirty-five
years, She has served Atlanta's finest
fried whiting, red velvet cake, and the best
sweet potato soufflé to ever touch a plate:: that
every Monday, She bakes Heaven
into buttery pastries (with fresh berries
in the frosting) for the bus driver to hand out
on his route, as each rider gets off:: & that once
upon a time, with just the smile
of Her eyes, She saved a runaway
named Mary, teetering above a river
of cars, from leaping off
the Lee Street Bridge.

II.

IT HAS ALSO BEEN SAID that God spins
on Fly Fridays at the Apache Café
& His Afro is perfect
(though we've never seen Him
pick it), dancing a boogie in His golden dashiki
each time He plays "As" by Stevie
Wonder, "Shining Star" by Earth, Wind & Fire,
or any cut by Chic:: that a surefire
way to feel His fury is to stand on His dance
floor without moving, which induces His Highest Truth
from the deejay booth—*What you come
round here for, if you ain't come
to dance?*—a Truth so high, it comes
in the form of a question.

III.

IT HAS ALSO BEEN SAID that God lives
in a certain church (which
there's no need to mention by name) but

Even when I knew their songs, they said
I sang off-key. *Now bow,*
now kneel, now chant, now pray: I stumbled
dizzily   into a sticky web
the gossips wove—*Was that for me?*
Among all of these things,
I had the hardest time finding God
there.

On Closing Woodruff Park, Atlanta (for renovation for the 1996 Summer Olympics)

exhaling...

       icicle-clad, sky-blue breath

   inhaling...

               sharp, cold metallic

abandonment...

They've closed Woodruff Park where, last summer,

    Brother Johnson, in a striped bow-tie

        one of the brothers from The Nation gave him

        at the shelter back in '87 (he was so proud),

        preached his daily sermon to a crowd

        of no fewer than two hundred

        about *the power of Black Nationalism*

        & how *Geronimo Pratt is still in prison*

        & *Mumia Abu Jamal still ain't free*; and

    Sister Mabel *Boydidyoucombyohairthismawnin?* Davis

       was always *makin sho the city clean*

       when all dem White folks n' Japs come in 1996.

       You don't want dem goin back n' tellin' dey people

       Atlanta's a nasty city wit trash all ovah da ground.

       I mean you wouldn't invite company 'round

yo house if you hadn't cleaned up, wouldya? unaware
of her pending eviction notice
as she picked up a policeman's
abandoned Dunkin' Donuts bag; and

Mister Haynes (he nothing to lose, I a friend to gain)
bet me lunch he could checkmate me
in ten moves (it only took seven)
& I bought him a sandwich at Michael's Deli.
Best meal I had since Hosea's dinnah last Christmas season.
Turkey & Swiss. *No pork. Brother Johnson say*
dat's blue-eyed devil food. With ridged corn chips.
Man, I ain't had dese in...

a luxury I guess
when you are homeless—
when your home
address is
Woodruff Park.

All that hair must be hot
I thought. But
it must be warm
in the winter (in this air
that hurts to breathe.)

I wonder
     if Black turns to blue
          when you're that cold,
     old, low & forgotten
by this progressive city of lofty,
     glass skyscrapers
          full of stonethrowers
     who've never walked a mile
even in their own shoes.

Holding the mayor's free
     one-way bus ticket
          to AnywhereButHere
     if you'll just sign this contract
that you'll never come back.

Heartless January
     shrilling
          like an angry woman
     You are nothing
in your ear.

I wonder
where they live
now

The Barbershop Philosopher's
1st Law of Social Mobility

Those in no hurry

to go

Anywhere

Usually

have no Where

to go.

Urban Percussions

Killed... I killed him with my own hands.

—Aime Cesaire

Tuesday, December 12, 1993

I sat at my window, gazing at the city—

bright lights, lasciviousness & lies,

sleek subway trains, and steel towers that soared

     to the sky.

In swoons I dug the swing

of Miles' horn ridin the high hat,

bathed in the subtle static

of my old phonograph.

The wintry wind whistled

a somber tune as a lone cloud

vanquished the moon.

Echoes of gunshots hung heavy

in the air, and somewhere

a mad drummer played his beats...

Yo, there's that cat Nat—

I lifted his rims a while back

4:23 on my wristpiece—A. M., that is—

the phone rang, and who could it be

        but Tracy

in herbal heights ramblin

bout her glittering dreams

of showbiz—ruby rings, candy-apple cars,

& scarlet sequined dresses. *Baby,*

I'm gonna be a star.

Miss Smile Brite 1979. I was

Miss Smile Brite 1979.

At the age of five I was live,

& I know *my face was destined*

         for magazine covers.

She'd had many lovers

tryin to sex her way to the top.

Then, on her voice, rained the patter

of teardrops—fallin & fallin.

Tracy's bawlin drowned the sounds

of Ice beatin his wife in the flat next door.

I could do no more than listen

as the voice on the other end

wailed of having no friends

and of being alone in this city

of being *so alone in this city…*

In the daylight some called her siditty

but only I knew of her vulnerability

in the night. *Come on over,* she said.

I need a shoulder

to cry on. Then, a dial tone...

So I slipped on my gear

made my way

toward the West side of town.

Caddy out front, brothas smokin blunts—

the dawn wrestled with the night.

The fiery ashes of a cigarette

lay dying on a stair, and somewhere

a mad drummer played his beats...

There's that pimp Kimp—

duped him for a dimebag of hemp...

Slapped fives and gave dap,

floored the gas but had a flat.

Wouldya believe on MLK?

Got out, locked my doors,

givin nods to the whores

packin it up for the night.

Went on trailed by a cop,

ducked into a doughnut shop

        & ordered my usual.

After done I made a run

two blocks west of Ashby

in the shadow of the rising sun.

Finally, I made it to Tracy's crib

on the West side of town.
Yo, there's that nig Pig,
from whose hoochie I took a swig...

On the West side of town
I took the elevator to the floor
where Tracy stayed.
And from somewhere
near the end of the hall played—
or so it seemed—
the blatant blare of trumpet screams.
On the fourth floor,
Tracy already stood in the door
of apartment G. Tracy was bawlin
as I was stallin, wonderin
what the problem could be.

Can I come in? In a daze, she nodded.
I poked and prodded
to find her trouble.
And she looked to the double beds
in her bedroom.
I didn't know what was in store
till I looked at the floor and saw
a pool of red.
My reflection in a pool, blood red.

Lying face-down on the carpet
was a brotha—dead.
I turned his face over

And it was me.
It was me.
It was me.

And somewhere
a mad drummer played his beats.
A dance with death
to the rhythm
of urban percussions.

III.

Unmanifesto (Notes on Post-Postcolonialism: a 3rd Draft in CP Time)

Yes, actually this is

another poem about race. (Maybe they all

are. (This time, the arrival ritual

is metaphor; next time, a primate; then, a grass

hut. Anything to show how natural

I am. (But hasn't my nature

always been the problem? (Am I being

too prosaic? (Is my directness

unsettling?))))) Try unsettling

America. Humor me. Start with Hawaii

& Alaska. Unmanifest

these destinies: Undo the Sioux,

the Iroquois, the Trail of Tears. Undo

me—each shackle. (Hint:

My grinning is not a sign

I'm into bondage.) Undo amber waves

of grain (I mean

the song) & the transcontinental

train, track upon track, each

railroad tie back to free

labor—Chinese, Chicano & other-
wise. Undo sands
across deserts. Undo ours
& centuries.   (But who can undo
when bound by Time's
linear contract? (which I am now

breaking.)) Undo the starless
Black futures of your science
fictions. Undo Blacklessness
on the Jetsons. Undo 3rd
World. Undo un-
namings of Kunta & Biafra.   Undo
uncivilized. (No, I mean
the concept.) Undo
these undoings: Navajo,
Inca, Aztec. Backtrack
across the Atlantic to the Gold

Coast. Let us critique you,
weigh you: Determine whether you're real
art.

Conjurewoman

Her locks are a swarm of black comets
streaming through ionized air. But her eyes: center

of my universe – twin suns blazing so brown
as to make brown iridescent. She makes alien

races envious. Her skin, a brown hymn. When God
made the line of her smile, Heaven broke

in two. Each eyelash, a chord bending in Muddy
Waters' hands; each blink, a blues song; each

sidelong look, a jook joint con-
cert. Her hips, an upright bass I want

to strum. Long. & slow. With my bow, and I do
mean deeply. Her walk, a wicked bassline

only the Devil could play. Each areola, a voodoo spell
I want to chant. Her curvatures

would make geometricians jealous. An hourglass
that walks, she leaves me

with no past. Which is to say:

I ain't ever seen another

woman.

Once, During an Eclipse, I Happened to Look into the Sun

while listening to her
lavender lips (with flaming auburn afro—
supernova of bossa nova
(in zodiacal cobalt earrings & lustrous moon-
    suit mini))

(while listening to her) blurb
some blue music—astrophonic/vibraphonic—
    about how her
        neighbor's3-storyatriumandnewEgyptianroom
    outshone her
        father's2-storyatriumandlackthereof
    & how her
        sequinedgownfromSierraLeonemaynotmakeitbackintimeforthe
            Governor'sball
    forcing her to wear
        somedomesticAnneKleinmassproductioninstead

(while listening to this) i noticed my proletarian reflection
    in the shallow inky pools
    of her eyes, looked at the metallic crescent
    hanging by Orion's belt

in the dusty purple sky
& wondered…

if i took her silver anklet
and tossed it at the moon,
would it clink?
or would it fall

onto deaf ears?

The Veil

—David, from James Baldwin's *Giovanni's Room*

There is something more to this photograph

than a groom & his best man

     posing

in white tuxedos with tails.

More than a wilting carnation

& matte-pink lipstick staining his lapel.

More than his lovely bride in white,

oblivious in this *mise en scene*,

barefoot in the lush green grass

midst melting ice nymphs, rich rumcake

& a carnival of carved fruit. Her arm is cut

off. (How can she love him

whom she can never truly

know?)   *Elle est tres ravissante*

et exotique—like someone else's

     dream;

something of a showpiece: a finely

crafted Beninese ivory bracelet,

an adornment, a bride.

A veil,

out of focus—Impressionistic, as if

by Monet or Pissarro. Champagne

& the mountains of darkening

      ivory clouds.

       .

There is something more to this

than the groom's asymmetric smile. His lost

gaze, down and slightly

to the left. Some thing less

      than God

Who is always there, but Who

we cannot see.

Here is some thing more than a brotherly

arm around his shoulder, now falling

about his waist. More than a dull

gold wedding band already

      slipping

off his hand. More than a groom

& his best friend: a veil (a love)?

Which can never be lifted.

Lovesong at the End of the World

Love, I have fallen
out of orbit, clutching only this blazing heart-
shaped chute. Even after you were the last
O_2 molecule in my vacuous universe, I inhaled
deeply. I consumed
you. By the time these echoes
of light reach you, I will be a forgotten con-
stellation of half-truths—a brazen horizon
fallen—a thousand starry bones tossed from your door
of diamond flame.

Will you forever behold me in this fractured
prison of light—even after I've drifted
light years away from you?

Why fossilize this moment
I've dreaded for so long? The end

*

Of the world. Will my unborn, too,
gather light in hollow mouths & blow

blue moons? Will the lunar winds forever moan
Etta James? Look, what can be more earnest than I
beating my cavernous chest till my fists

shatter into rings of ice? My forsaken love
blossoms for you like a monstrous
mushroom cloud. I loved you wholly,
the only way I knew how. With my whole
heart—even the darkest part, which is the black
hole that softly devoured
you

Day Negative 7

16 May 2000. He is flying (or falling) – no – lying
to himself. Death traps his breath in a lode-
stone BOX (N.) →
>   corner: a predicament from which
>   graceful escape is impossible
Who owns the air? the voice asks. *Who,
the Earth?* He
>   fights God with eight
translucent arms. Thick yellow fog
is boiling. Boils
>   for eyes. Swirling black columns
of smoke rise like stilts as he walks
Who owns the flowers? When he climbs
into the coffin, Venus
flytraps of lightning
open: knock-knock. All bone. *Who owns
the sea?* Can you?   Another black O
on his thigh. A pair, a MOON (N.) →
>   a small body in orbit about a planet

(*piano*)   *I am coming back.*

K.S., night sweats, an opera
of coughing. A coffin. Too short. *Pulse?*

*

Pulse? One hundred
thousand black ants scurry
through the artery. No
escape. *Who owns this*
body? Stars
over Miami. Hands
in every crevice. *Who owns*
light? Reach. No flowers but
(pianissimo) *I am coming back soon.*
gravestones. First
son. Last
light. First
love. Last
LUST (N.) →
                Deadly seven.
Future. Face it:
A bouquet of injections.
ER.   Stretcher.
Votre statu, monsieur?
Your status?

90

A Sharecropper's Pantoum

—for a dry season

The drug cocktails that have slashed the mortality rate of HIV-positive people in the U.S. and Western Europe are all but non-existent in Haiti. [O]nly 3 to 4 percent of people with AIDS [there] have access to the newest drugs.

—Alfredo S. Lanier, *The Chicago Tribune*, 2003

Hauling this pine box on a black Chevrolet,

I pray to a candle at the end of its wick.

White burial clothes in a garbage bag,

I ride for a place to die.

I pray to a candle at the end of its wick

on the mud road home from Port-au-Prince

and ride toward a place to die

where mangoes hang and sugarcane turns.

By the dust road home from Port-au-Prince,

I am a black skeleton—6 feet tall, yet 90 pounds—

where mangoes hang and sugarcane burns.

I turned the earth before I got this thing.

A lesioned skeleton—a rainbow tall, now 70 pounds—

I dream across the waters and of the miracles there

and turn to earth in the jaws of this thing:

eyes—black holes, lungs—green clouds.

Dreaming across the waters and of the miracles there,
white burial clothes in a garbage bag,
eyes—black holes, lungs—green clouds,
I haul my pine coffin in a black Chevrolet.

Of Ash & Dust

—for the flight crew of STS-107, Space Shuttle *Columbia* (Rick
Husband, William McCool, Michael Anderson, Ilan Ramon,
Kalpana Chawla, David Brown, and Laurel Clark)

I. 1981

A Black Second

Lieutenant & his squadron

crowd the Magnavox to watch

Columbia, a virgin flight—shining

against cobalt blue, even confined in this

13-inch box, throttling atop a temple

of flame to Heaven. His pulse

races   as rocket boosters

deploy; fall; parachute—just short

of angels back to Earth & the spent

external tank breaks

away   as planned—

splashing where ocean

praises sky. While the shuttle

hurtles into the holiness

of black, kissing the starry hem

of God. The lieutenant's eyes: Wide

as two black worlds. What a dream

to live &

die like this:

II. 2003

Now his own trip into outer

space—what a marvelous

view. Every 90 minutes, the Great Wall

of China, the Ganges

River, the Sahara, and Death

Valley—a falling

without falling. Over

& over: a new sun, a new moon, a new

Earth. 255 times before

the final descent.   An alarm: Boards

& boards of flashing red lights. One after another, a cosmic wildfire.

WARNING WARNING and sensors & panic, bulging of eyes and

smashing of panels. *Houston, Houston, the whole cabin's quaking.* Stars &

stripes & shockwaves in plasma. *I can't feel my hands* and cursing & praying

in Hebrew & Hindi. *This can't be happening/ My daughters are waiting/ The

stars are behind us.* Just 15 minutes from kebabs & kugel, from sand

between toes, from Yoel's bar mitzvah. *Mayday Mayday, if you're there, Jesus,

answer!* Depressurization. Circuitry burning. *I see Jimi Hendrix/ See,

Yahweh, I'm kosher/ I pray that my ashes are blown to the ocean   We've

lost all power/ Temperature's rising.* Halos of fuel, the whole sky is splitting.

*I will die clutching this relic from Auschwitz. The light is so blinding. My God,

California!* Clutching & trembling & thunder & lightning: a great flash of

flame as hearts beco(m)———

About the Author

Born in Atlanta, poet M. Ayodele Heath is a graduate of the MFA program at New England College. Heath's honors include a 2009 Dorothy Rosenberg Prize and a McEver Visiting Chair in Writing at Georgia Tech. He has been awarded fellowships from Cave Canem, Summer Poetry at Idyllwild, and the Caversham Centre for Writers & Artists in South Africa and received a grant in Literary Arts from the Atlanta Bureau for Cultural Affairs. His work has appeared or is forthcoming in: *Crab Orchard Review*, *diode*, *Mississippi Review*, *Callaloo*, *The New York Quarterly*, *Chattahoochee Review*, and *Mythium*, as well as featured in anthologies including *Poetry Slam: the Competitive Art of Performance Poetry* (2000), *Java Monkey Speaks Anthology I* (2004), and *My South: a People, a Place, a World All Its Own* (2005).

Made in the USA
Charleston, SC
28 March 2014